"Please join me in welcoming the lovely ladies of the Beaubaxtons Academy of Magic!"

—Albus Dumbledore, *Harry Potter and the Goblet of Fire*

"Blimey, it's him. Viktor Krum."
—Ron Weasley, *Harry Potter and the Goblet of Fire*

"Eternal glory. That is what awaits the student who wins the Triwizard Tournament. But to do this that student must survive three tasks. Three extremely dangerous tasks."

—Albus Dumbledore, *Harry Potter and the Goblet of Fire*

"Alastor Moody: Ex-Auror, Ministry malcontent, and your new Defense Against the Dark Arts teacher."

—Alastor Moody, *Harry Potter and the Goblet of Fire*

GEORGE: "Ready, Fred?"

FRED: "Ready, George."

FRED AND GEORGE: "Bottoms up."

— *Harry Potter and the Goblet of Fire*

"Harry Potter!"

—Albus Dumbledore, *Harry Potter and the Goblet of Fire*

"You're the juicy news! What quirks lurk beneath those rosy cheeks, what mysteries do the muscles mask, does courage lie beneath those curls? In short, what makes a champion tick?"

—Rita Skeeter, *Harry Potter and the Goblet of Fire*

HERMIONE: "How are you feeling? Okay? The key is to concentrate. After that you just have to—"

HARRY: "Battle a dragon."

—*Harry Potter and the Goblet of Fire*

"I look like my Great Aunt Tessie!"

—Ron Weasley, *Harry Potter and the Goblet of Fire*

"Is that Hermione Granger? With Viktor Krum?"

—Padma Patil, *Harry Potter and the Goblet of Fire*

PADMA: "Are you going to ask me to dance or not?"
RON: "No."

—Harry Potter and the Goblet of Fire

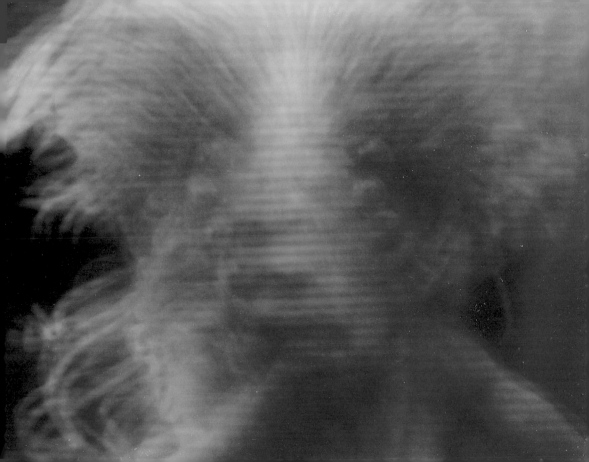

"There aren't merpeople in the Black Lake, are there?"

—Harry Potter, *Harry Potter and the Goblet of Fire*

"In the maze, you'll find no dragons or creatures of the deep. Instead you'll face something even more challenging. You see, people change in the maze. Oh, find the cup if you can, but be very wary, you could just lose yourselves along the way."

—Albus Dumbledore, *Harry Potter and the Goblet of Fire*

THOMAS RIDDLE
1880 - 1943

...RY RIDDLE
1883 - 1913

TOM MARVOLO
RIDDLE
1915 - 1943

"I've been here before. In a dream. Cedric, we have to get back to the cup. Now!"

—Harry Potter, *Harry Potter and the Goblet of Fire*

"Don't you turn your back on me, Harry Potter!
I want you to look at me when I kill you!"

—Voldemort, *Harry Potter and the Goblet of Fire*

"Today, we acknowledge a really terrible loss. Cedric Diggory was, as you all know, exceptionally hardworking, infinitely fair-minded, and most importantly a fierce, fierce friend. Now I think, therefore, that you have the right to know exactly how he died. You see, Cedric Diggory was murdered. By Lord Voldemort."

—Albus Dumbledore, *Harry Potter and the Goblet of Fire*